TRAUMA INFORMED INTERVENTION

Healing, Resilience, and Compassion

John Baba

CONTENTS

INTRODUCTION

We take a thorough tour of the field of trauma-informed intervention in this book. We will look at the complex web of trauma, its enormous effects on people, and the considerate, empathic techniques that can open the door to empowerment and healing.

CHAPTER 1: TRAUMA UNVEILED

Defining Trauma: What Is Trauma, And How Does It Manifest In Individuals' Lives?

Trauma is a complex, intensely personal event that can take many different forms in people's life. To properly understand trauma, we must examine its meaning, its manifestations, and the devastating effects it has on individuals who experience it.

Recognizing trauma

Trauma can be roughly defined as a psychological and emotional reaction to a distressing or destructive incident or series of events. The tendency of trauma to exceed a person's capability for effective coping distinguishes it from regular stress or adversity. Trauma frequently happens when a person feels as though their physical or mental health is under danger, or when they observe someone else suffering harm.

Different Traumas

There are many different types of trauma, and each has its own distinct traits:

Trauma that results in physical harm to the body is referred to as a physical trauma. Car crashes, slips and falls, and physical assault are a few examples.

*Psychological or Emotional Trauma: Emotional trauma is frequently correlated with upsetting life events including the loss of a loved one, divorce, or emotional abuse. It may cause severe emotional anguish and have an impact on mental health.

Trauma that occurs during key phases of a child's development is referred to as developmental trauma, and it can have long-lasting impacts. Developmental trauma can be brought on by abuse, neglect, or the death of a caregiver.

*Complex trauma is brought on by repeated exposure to traumatic events, which frequently take place in the context of interpersonal interactions. Domestic violence, persistent child abuse, and captivity are a few examples.

*Secondary trauma, sometimes referred to as vicarious trauma, occurs when people are exposed to trauma inadvertently through their jobs or relationships. Professionals who frequently see trauma in others, such as first responders, therapists, and carers, are affected.

Signs and Symptoms of Trauma

Trauma can appear in people's lives in a variety of ways, and its repercussions aren't always immediately obvious. among their frequent signs are:

*Psychological Symptoms: Trauma can cause symptoms including dissociation, anxiety, depression, flashbacks, and nightmares. People may have trouble controlling their emotions and may constantly feel afraid or helpless.

*Bodily Symptoms: Trauma frequently has bodily effects, such as chronic pain, sleep abnormalities, and digestive problems. The emotional toll of trauma might be made worse by these physical symptoms.

*Behavior Modifications: Trauma can alter behavior, leading to withdrawal from social situations, substance misuse, or self-destructive actions.

*Relationship Challenges: Trauma can cause relationships to become strained as a result of issues with intimacy, trust, and communication. It may be difficult for survivors to establish new relationships or to keep up with old ones.

Trauma can impair cognitive functioning, which can result in issues with focus, memory, and decision-making.

It's critical to remember that trauma is a highly personalized experience, and that each person's experience will appear differently. Additionally, the effects of trauma may not be seen right away; they may take time to manifest, often years after the traumatic occurrence.

The first step in offering effective trauma-informed intervention is realizing the complexity of trauma. We will explore further into the neuroscience of trauma, the foundations of trauma-informed care, and methods for assisting people on their path to empowerment in the following chapters of this book.

Types Of Trauma: Exploring Different Categories Of Trauma.

We examined the definition of trauma and how it manifests in people's lives in the previous chapter. We will examine the many classifications or forms of trauma that individuals may encounter in further detail in this chapter. For trauma-informed intervention options to be tailored to the specific needs of survivors, it is crucial to comprehend these various categories.

1. Acute trauma

A single traumatic event or a string of events that are closely related and take place quickly are referred to as acute trauma. It frequently conjures up images of an abrupt, unanticipated, and startling experience. Car crashes, natural disasters, physical assaults, and robbery are a few instances of acute trauma. Acute trauma may cause immediate distress, but it also has the potential to have long-term psychological and emotional repercussions.

2. Persistent Trauma:

When a person is continuously exposed to upsetting or dangerous conditions over a lengthy period of time, chronic trauma, often referred to as persistent or ongoing trauma, develops. This kind of trauma is frequently linked to continuing physical, emotional, or sexual abuse, spousal abuse, or living in a violent, unstable, or neglectful environment. The impacts of chronic trauma can compound over time and affect a person's physical, mental, and emotional health.

3. Compound Trauma:

Multiple traumatic events that frequently take place in the setting of interpersonal interactions are included in the category of "complex trauma." When it strikes people while they are going through crucial stages of early development, it is frequently referred to as "Developmental Trauma." Childhood traumas like physical, emotional, or sexual abuse, neglect, or being raised in a dysfunctional family structure can all lead to complex trauma. Complex trauma survivors may experience a variety of emotional and interpersonal difficulties.

4. Repetitive Trauma

Vicarious trauma, sometimes referred to as secondary trauma, is when people unintentionally suffer the trauma of others. This is typical among professionals and caregivers who have regular contact with trauma survivors, including therapists, medical staff, emergency personnel, and social workers. Constant exposure to the traumatic experiences of others can result in symptoms such as emotional anguish, burnout, and compassion fatigue that are comparable to those experienced by trauma survivors themselves.

5. Trauma from the past or across generations:

Trauma that has been passed down through the generations is referred to as historical or intergenerational trauma. It happens when the trauma suffered by a previous generation continues to have an impact on the lives of succeeding generations. Examples include the trauma passed down through generations in communities impacted by genocide, enslavement, or colonization. Recognizing how trauma affects marginalized communities on a structural and social level requires an understanding of historical trauma.

6. Trauma based on culture and identity:

Trauma based on culture and identity is a result of prejudice, racism, and oppression that targets individuals or groups based on their race, ethnicity, gender, sexual orientation, or other identifiers. These situations may have long-term psychological and social repercussions, which can exacerbate existing inequities in mental health and wellbeing.

It is critical to understand that people may go through multiple types of trauma at once or throughout the course of their lives. Interventions informed by trauma should be sensitive to these differences and customized to meet the unique needs and experiences of survivors. The principles of trauma-informed care and evidence-based approaches to supporting people who have gone through various types of trauma will be covered in the upcoming chapters.

The Neurobiology Of Trauma: Understanding How Trauma Affects The Brain And Body.

Trauma affects people profoundly on a

neurobiological level as well as emotionally and psychologically. This chapter will examine the effects of trauma on the brain and body, illuminating the complex interplay between the mind and physiological reactions.

1. How Trauma Affects the Brain

The brain reacts quickly and adaptively when a person suffers a traumatic incident. The threat signal is sent by the amygdala, a brain area involved in processing emotions, and the hypothalamus then triggers the body's stress response mechanism. Stress hormones like cortisol and adrenaline are released as a result, preparing the body to react to danger—often referred to as the "fight or flight" reaction.

However, this response system can become dysregulated in situations of severe or persistent stress. Some of the main impacts of trauma on the brain include the following:

*Hypervigilance: Even in non-threatening circumstances, trauma survivors may continue to be on high alert and continually on the lookout for potential hazards.

Traumatic memories may be processed differently in the brain, making them extremely vivid and challenging to erase. Flashbacks and bothersome thoughts may result from this.

*Emotional Dysregulation: Trauma can impair the brain's capacity to control emotions, resulting in ferocious mood swings and a challenge controlling emotional responses.

2. The Stress Response Mechanism

The stress response system in the body is triggered by trauma, and this can have significant impacts on physical health. Chronic system activation may result in:

*Immune System Impairment: Long-term stress compromises immunity, leaving people more prone to sickness.

*Cardiovascular Problems: The production of stress hormones can aggravate hypertension and cardiac conditions.

Irritable bowel syndrome and other gastrointestinal problems can be brought on by long-term stress.

Trauma can increase a person's pain sensitivity, which might result in chronic pain disorders.

3. The Nervous System's Effect:

Trauma can cause the autonomic nervous system, which controls unconscious body processes, to become dysregulated. Symptoms caused by this include:

*Dissociation: Trauma victims who go through periods of dissociation may feel cut off from their bodies or the current moment.

*Numbness or Hypervigilance: As the nervous system tries to adjust to perceived threats, people may oscillate between emotional numbness and hypervigilance.

4. Modifications to Brain Structure:

Chronic trauma has been linked to structural changes in the brain, particularly in regions involved in memory, emotion regulation, and stress response, according to research. The signs and long-term repercussions of trauma may be made worse by these changes.

For trauma-informed intervention, it is essential to comprehend the neurobiology of trauma. It emphasizes the physical effects of trauma and the value of holistic care that takes into account both the emotional and physical needs of trauma recovery. We will examine trauma-informed therapeutic modalities and how they can assist people in recovering from the neurobiological impacts of trauma in the following chapters.

CHAPTER 2: THE POWER OF EMPATHY

Empathy And Trauma: How Cultivating Empathy Is The Cornerstone Of Trauma-Informed Care.

Not only is empathy a quality of effective caregivers, but it also serves as the cornerstone of trauma-informed care. In this chapter, we'll look at the significant contributions empathy makes to the healing and emancipation of trauma survivors.

Defining Empathy

The capacity for empathy is the capacity to comprehend and experience another person's feelings. It entails not only being aware of another person's emotional state but also reacting in a way that shows concern, sympathy, and support. Empathy is a lifeline for trauma survivors who can use it to feel seen, heard, and accepted.

Empathy's Importance in Trauma-Informed Care

*Building Trust: Because of their history of abuse or betrayal, trauma survivors frequently struggle with issues of trust. The development of empathy fosters a secure and receptive environment where survivors can start to open up and heal.

*Validation: A strong type of validation is to be heard and understood. The emotions, experiences, and reality of the trauma experienced by survivors are validated by empathetic responses. The self-criticism and self-blame that frequently accompany trauma can be offset by this affirmation.

*Getting Rid of Shame and Isolation: Shame and isolation are common emotions among trauma survivors. Empathy reduces these thoughts by demonstrating that survivors are not alone in their problems.

*Communication Improvement: Healthy, open discussions between survivors and caregivers or therapists are fostered by listening and communicating with empathy. This makes it easier for survivors to communicate their needs and experiences.

Empathy Development in Trauma-Informed Care

Empathy requires a fundamental ability called active listening. Therapists and caregivers should practice focused, nonjudgmental listening and show a sincere interest in the survivor's story.

*Avoiding Judgment: Empathy necessitates putting aside one's preconceptions or judgments. It's important to acknowledge that each survivor's experience is distinct and that their emotional reactions are legitimate.

*Recognizing Triggers: When dealing with trauma survivors, caregivers should be aware of possible triggers and act delicately when they occur. Retraumatization must be avoided.

Empathy entails keeping room for survivors' emotions without becoming overstimulated or retaliatory. Caregivers need to be capable of self-regulation in order to do this.

Training in trauma-informed care is important for professionals and caregivers to better understand the effects of trauma and the most effective ways to respond sympathetically.

The Function of Self-Care in Caregiving

Offering emotional support to trauma survivors can be taxing. Self-care must be prioritized by caregivers and professionals if they want to keep their empathy and avoid burnout. Regular supervision, counselling, and looking for assistance from peers or mentors are just a few examples of self-care techniques.

In essence, successful trauma-informed treatment is based on empathy, which is both a talent and a mentality. It is the acceptance of another person's suffering and the dedication to accompanying them on their path to recovery and empowerment. We will examine practical methods and strategies that use empathy as a compass in trauma intervention in the ensuing chapters.

The Role Of Compassion: The Essential Ingredient In Building Trust And Safety.

A potent and crucial component of trauma-informed care is compassion. Together, they lay the groundwork for building a community of trust and safety for trauma survivors. It goes hand in hand with empathy. In this chapter, we'll examine how compassion aids in the healing process and plays a part in

trauma intervention.

What Is Compassion?

More than only having empathy or comprehending another person's suffering, compassion also entails a strong wish to lessen that suffering. It is the drive to intervene to relieve someone else's suffering or discomfort. The "action" of compassion is frequently referred to as coming after the "feeling" of empathy.

Compassion in Trauma-Informed Care: The Critical Role

Compassion is a crucial component in developing trust with trauma survivors. Survivors are more likely to feel protected and share their stories when they believe that caregivers genuinely care about their well-being.

*Creating Safety: Vulnerability and insecurity are common struggles for trauma survivors. Compassion creates a secure emotional environment where survivors can relax and start to heal.

*Empowerment: Caring for survivors with compassion helps them regain control of their lives. Change and healing might be sped up by knowing that someone is willing to help and care for them.

*Reducing Shame: Compassion aids in lessening the shame that frequently follows trauma. Survivors are less prone to hold themselves responsible for what happened when they are shown compassion and respect.

Compassion Development in Trauma-Informed Care

*Self-Compassion: Professionals and caregivers alike must first learn to show compassion to themselves. This entails being kind to oneself and accepting the possibility that working with trauma survivors may have an emotional cost on them as well.

*Empathetic Attunement: Empathetic attunement to the emotional condition of the survivor is the first step in developing compassion. Caretakers should make an effort to comprehend the survivor's viewpoint and emotional requirements.

*Acceptance without judgment: Compassion entails welcoming survivors without passing judgment on their deeds, feelings, or pasts. This acceptance demonstrates that they are respected for who they are as people.

*Validation: It's kind to acknowledge the feelings and experiences of survivors. They feel heard and understood when their sorrow and grief are acknowledged.

*Supporting Autonomy: Compassionate care honors the choices and autonomy of survivors. It incorporates cooperation instead than imposition, allowing survivors to choose their own course for healing.

*Setting Boundaries: To safeguard both themselves and the survivors, compassionate caregivers must set clear boundaries. Respecting professional standards or going against one's personal bounds is not what compassion entails.

The Consequences of Compassion

In addition to helping survivors, compassion has a positive knock-on impact that affects the entire community. When survivors feel compassion, they are more inclined to show it to others, creating an environment conducive to understanding and support.

We will examine how empathy and compassion might be incorporated into certain trauma-informed therapies in the chapters that follow, paving the road for survivors to recover and reclaim their lives.

Active Listening: Mastering The Art Of Listening To Create Connections.

Active listening is a fundamental skill in trauma-informed care, and it plays a pivotal role in establishing connections with trauma survivors. In this chapter, we will delve into the art of active listening, its importance in trauma intervention, and techniques to hone this crucial skill.

Defining Active Listening

Active listening is a dynamic and intentional form of listening. It involves not only hearing the words spoken by another person but also understanding their emotions, perspectives, and needs. Active listening goes beyond passive hearing; it requires engagement and a genuine desire to comprehend the speaker's experiences.

The Importance of Active Listening in Trauma-Informed Care

*Validation: Active listening communicates to survivors that their experiences and emotions are valid and worthy of attention. This validation is crucial in reducing the shame and self-doubt often associated with trauma.

*Empathy: Active listening fosters empathy by allowing caregivers to immerse themselves in the survivor's narrative. This deep understanding helps caregivers provide more empathetic and compassionate responses.

*Building Trust: When survivors feel heard and

understood, trust is cultivated. Active listening is a primary tool for establishing a safe and trusting therapeutic relationship.

*Facilitating Expression: Trauma survivors may find it challenging to express their thoughts and emotions. Active listening encourages them to articulate their experiences, facilitating the healing process.

Techniques for Mastering Active Listening

*Give Your Full Attention: When engaging with a survivor, eliminate distractions and focus your attention entirely on them. Maintain eye contact, use open body language, and show that you are fully present.

*Use Verbal and Non-Verbal Cues: Nodding, affirmative statements (e.g., "I understand," "Tell me more"), and reflective comments (e.g., "It sounds like you're feeling...") convey that you are actively listening.

*Ask Open-Ended Questions: Encourage survivors to share more about their experiences by asking open-ended questions that prompt reflection and elaboration.

*Paraphrase and Summarize: Periodically paraphrase or summarize what the survivor has shared to ensure you have correctly understood their perspective. This also reinforces that you are listening attentively.

*Avoid Interrupting or Rushing: Allow survivors to speak at their own pace, even if there are pauses or moments of silence. Avoid the temptation to fill these gaps.

*Show Empathy and Validation: Express empathy and validation for the survivor's emotions and experiences. Use phrases like "I can imagine how that must have felt," or "It's completely natural to feel that way."

*Avoid Judgment: Suspend judgment and remain non-judgmental, even if you disagree with the survivor's viewpoint or choices. Remember that your role is to support, not judge.

*Reflect on Your Responses: After the conversation, take time to reflect on your responses. Consider whether you demonstrated active listening and how you can improve in future interactions.

The Healing Power of Active Listening

Active listening is not just a skill; it is a profound act of compassion and respect. It empowers survivors to share their stories, reduces their sense of isolation, and aids in the process of healing. By mastering the art of active listening, caregivers and professionals can create deep and meaningful connections with trauma survivors, paving the way for recovery and empowerment. In the upcoming chapters, we will explore how active listening can be integrated into various trauma-informed interventions

CHAPTER 3: THE TRAUMA-INFORMED APPROACH

Core Principles: Key Principles Of Trauma-Informed Care.

Trauma-informed care is a concept and strategy that acknowledges the pervasive effects of trauma on people and communities. It is not just a set of tools. We will examine the fundamentals of trauma-informed care in this chapter, giving readers a solid understanding of how to build environments that are encouraging and healing.

1. Safety as the Base:

The foundation of trauma-informed care is safety. Traumatized people frequently have increased sensitivity to threats, whether they are genuine or imagined. Creating a secure environment requires that you:

*Put mental and physical safety first.

*Recognize potential triggers and try to prevent retraumatization.
*Establish credibility by continuously exhibiting dependability and predictability.

2. Reputation for Integrity and Openness:

For trauma survivors who may have endured betrayal or abuse, reliability is essential. The significance of: is emphasized by trauma-informed care.

*Honesty and openness in all dealings.
*Clear communication regarding procedures and expectations.
*Preserving moral principles and boundaries in the workplace.

3. Peer Assistance and Cooperation:

Peer support and collaboration are crucial components of trauma-informed care. This entails:

*Involving survivors in their recovery as active partners.
*Encouraging a sense of community and belonging.
*Encouraging service providers to work together to provide full support.

4. Voice, Choice, and Empowerment:

Trauma-informed care respects the autonomy of

survivors and gives them the power to decide how to proceed with their healing. This comprises:

*Whenever possible, giving survivors a choice and letting them have a say in their treatment.
*Encouraging survivors to speak up and share their wants, beliefs, and issues.
*Acknowledging that each survivor's road to recovery is different and that they are the foremost authorities on their own experiences.

5. Cultural humility and sensitivity:

As trauma affects people from many backgrounds, cultural competence is essential to trauma-informed care. Important factors include:

*Recognizing and honoring cultural customs and differences.
*Avoiding prejudices and assumptions.
*Seeking out ongoing instruction and training in cultural humility.

6. Strengths-based perspective and resilience

Survivors are seen as resiliant and capable of progress in trauma-informed care. This rule focuses on:

*Recognizing the abilities, capabilities, and resiliency of survivors.
*Putting more emphasis on people's strengths than

their weaknesses.
*Encouraging post-traumatic development and healing.

7. Understanding and Awareness of Trauma:

A thorough grasp of the impacts of trauma is a cornerstone of trauma-informed care. This comprises:

*Realizing how common trauma is and how it affects both physical and emotional health.
*Include trauma education in professional development and daily work.
*By careful use of words, attitudes, and actions, preventing retraumatization.

8. Resilience and Flexibility:

Care that has been shaped by trauma is adaptable and sensitive to the changing needs of survivors. This entails:

*Modifying interventions to accommodate a person's unique requirements and preferences.
*Being receptive to criticism and modifying strategies as necessary.
assessing and enhancing trauma-informed practices continuously.

9. Holistic wellness and health

Trauma-informed care understands that recovery goes beyond only treating the symptoms of the trauma. It consists of:

*Encouraging mental, emotional, and physical well.
*Implementing trauma-informed practices in systems such as healthcare, education, and others.

10. Social advocacy and justice:

Trauma-informed care addresses systemic problems in addition to individual rehabilitation. This comprises:

*Advocating for measures and procedures that support survivors and lessen trauma.
*Acknowledging the effects of societal injustices and pursuing social justice.

By adhering to these fundamental ideas, caregivers, professionals, and organizations can develop settings and programs that empower trauma victims, encourage healing, and advance the larger goal of lessening the occurrence and effects of trauma on society. We shall examine how these ideas can be used in various contexts and locations in the chapters that follow.

Understanding Triggers: Identifying And Managing Trauma Triggers.

Trauma survivors frequently struggle with triggers —sensory encounters, ideas, or circumstances that bring up uncomfortable memories and feelings related to their trauma. This chapter will examine the idea of triggers, their effects on survivors, and methods for locating and controlling them.

What Are Trauma Triggers?

Trauma triggers are stimuli that cause people to recall their traumatic experiences and relive the related feelings, sensations, and memories. Both internal (thoughts or emotions) and exterior (sensory cues or circumstances) factors can act as triggers. Common triggers include certain words or phrases, scents, images, sounds, and even specific dates or anniversaries.

Effects of Triggers

Triggers can significantly affect trauma survivors:

*Emotional distress can result from triggers that cause strong feelings like fear, rage, anxiety, or grief.

*Vivid memories that make survivors feel as though they are reliving the traumatic incident are common.

*Physical Reactions: Triggers can cause physical symptoms like accelerated breathing, increased heart rate, and perspiration.

*Avoidance: In an effort to avoid triggers, survivors may withdraw socially or steer clear of situations, which lowers their quality of life.

Recognizing Triggers

A crucial first step in trauma-informed care is recognizing triggers. Together, caregivers, therapists, and survivors can pinpoint and comprehend these triggers. Following are some techniques for locating triggers:

*Encourage survivors to speak openly about their triggers and experiences. In these discussions, attentive listening is crucial.

*Trauma History: A thorough understanding of the trauma history of the survivor can help identify potential triggers.

*Patterns of Reactivity: Track the survivor's emotional and physical reactivity to various circumstances or stimuli.

*Trauma-Informed Assessment: To systematically identify triggers, use trauma-informed assessment instruments and interviews.

Controlling Triggers

The next step is to create ways to manage and cope with triggers after they have been identified:

Teaching survivors grounding skills will help them remain rooted in the present when they are triggered. These could entail employing sensory stimuli, practicing awareness, or deep breathing.

*Cognitive behavioral therapy (CBT) can assist survivors in reframing their attitudes and reactions to triggers, so lessening the emotional effect of those events.

*Exposure therapy can help survivors become less sensitive to triggers over time by exposing them to them progressively in safe and encouraging circumstances.

*Safety Planning: Work with survivors to develop safety plans that specify what to do in case of triggers. This may entail locating secure areas or contacts.

*Encourage people to engage in self-care activities that help them control their emotions, such as exercise, meditation, and following a regular schedule.

*Supportive Care: Trauma-focused therapy, such as

Dialectical Behavior Therapy (DBT) or Eye Movement Desensitization and Reprocessing (EMDR), can be successful in treating triggers.

*Medication: Medication may be administered in some circumstances to treat symptoms brought on by triggers, such as anxiety or panic attacks.

Creating Environments That Are Trigger Sensitive

Making trigger-sensitive surroundings is also vital in trauma-informed care. This entails:

*In therapy or educational settings, clearly stating trigger warnings.
*recognizing possible triggers in the immediate surroundings (such as sensory sensations).
*observing the limits and trigger-management preferences of survivors.
Trauma-informed treatment involves an ongoing process of understanding, recognizing, and addressing trauma triggers. Caregivers and professionals can offer a supportive and empowering environment for healing by collaborating with survivors and employing trigger-sensitive procedures.

Safety And Trust: Building A Secure Foundation For Intervention.

The healing process in trauma-informed care

depends on establishing a setting that values safety and encourages trust. The importance of safety and trust, their importance, and methods for building and sustaining them throughout the intervention process are all covered in this chapter.

The Importance of Trust and Safety

1. As a Foundation, Safety:

The cornerstone on which trauma rehabilitation is constructed is safety. Safety is crucial because trauma survivors frequently have a greater sense of vulnerability and danger. People are more inclined to participate in therapy and be honest about their experiences when they feel protected.

2. The Healing Catalyst: Trust

In trauma intervention, trust is a healing-inducing catalyst. Gaining survivors' confidence, respect, and sense of value can have a big impact on how likely they are to discuss their traumatizing experiences, feelings, and vulnerabilities.

4. Building Safety and Trust: Strategies

Make a Safe Space in Your Home:

Make sure the physical setting where intervention takes place is secure and devoid of potential triggers. Think about elements like privacy, comfort, and sensory inputs that could influence the survivor's perception of safety.

5. Establish Limits:

To establish a predictable and secure environment, establish clear and consistent boundaries. Respect the boundaries and preferences of survivors, and let them know if anything changes or veers from the accepted course of action.

6. Trauma-Informed Evaluation:

A trauma-informed evaluation that takes into account the survivor's needs, triggers, and history should be the first step in the therapeutic process. This demonstrates your respect for their individual perspectives.

7. Communication and openness

Encourage direct and truthful communication. Be open and honest about the objectives, procedures, and potential difficulties of the intervention. Respond to inquiries honestly and take care of any issues that may surface.

8. Playful Listening

Actively listen to others to demonstrate empathy and understanding. Demonstrate your whole attention to the survivor's needs and experiences by being fully present.

9. Freedom and Choice:

Give survivors the chance to decide on their own care and rehabilitation. Encourage children to participate in decisions that have an impact on their life.

10. Reliability and consistency:

Be dependable and consistent in your dealings. Be on time and fulfill your obligations. By fostering predictability, consistency fosters trust.

11. Respect for Individuality:

Respect the survivor's independence and capacity for making decisions. Keep your own agenda and opinions to yourself. Instead, assist and support their decision-making.

12. Cultural sensitivity:

By being conscious of and respecting the survivor's cultural background, beliefs, and customs, demonstrate cultural competence and humility. This fosters trust by demonstrating respect.

Training that is trauma-informed:

Continue to educate yourself and your team about the principles and procedures of trauma-informed treatment. By receiving regular training, you can make sure that your strategy follows trauma-informed concepts.

Recognize that carers and professionals require assistance and self-care in order to keep up their capacity to deliver safe and reliable care. The process of establishing safety and trust might be endangered by burnout.

Use language that is trauma-informed to minimize stigmatization, condemnation, or victim-blaming. The language you choose can have a big impact on how survivors interpret your intentions and the environment's safety.

It takes continual work to establish safety and trust in trauma-informed treatment, but doing so is an investment in the recovery and well-being of the survivor. Caregivers and professionals build a solid foundation for trauma response and recovery by putting safety first and encouraging trust.

CHAPTER 4: THE LIFELONG IMPACT OF CHILDHOOD TRAUMA

Adverse Childhood Experiences (Aces):

The long-term consequences of early trauma.

Adverse Childhood Experiences (ACEs) are a group of distressing situations and events that happen to kids. This chapter will examine what ACEs are, how common they are, and the deep and long-lasting effects they have on people throughout the course of their lives.

Adverse Childhood Experiences (ACEs) Definition

ACEs are a broad category of unfavorable situations and occurrences that can seriously harm a child's wellbeing. The Centers for Disease Control and Prevention (CDC) and Kaiser Permanente's initial ACEs study discovered the 10 categories of ACEs listed below:

*Bodily abuse is when a caregiver or other authority

figure intentionally causes bodily pain or injury to the child.

*Child sexual exploitation or non-consensual sexual activity is sexual abuse.

*Continual humiliation, rejection, or harsh criticism are examples of emotional abuse that a kid may experience.

*Neglect: When a child's fundamental needs—such as those for food, housing, affection, and supervision —are repeatedly unmet.

*Substance addiction in the home: The child's family member suffers with abusing drugs or alcohol.

*Mental illness in the family: A family member of the child has a mental illness that materially reduces their ability to function or quality of life.

*Child witnesses physical abuse or ongoing arguments between the adults in the home when there is domestic violence.

*Parental divorce or separation: If the child's parents split up, it may cause the family to fall apart.

*Household member in prison: The family of the child is faced with both emotional and practical difficulties because a family member in prison.

*Chronic disease or disability: A household member or a child is dealing with persistent physical or mental health issues.

the frequency of ACEs

ACEs occur more frequently than one might think. According to research, a sizable fraction of the populace has gone through one or more ACEs. The probability of unfavorable outcomes is increased by the cumulative nature of ACEs, where many events frequently co-occur.

The Long-Term Effects of ACEs

ACEs have extensive and long-lasting effects on a person's life. These effects consist of:

*Physical Health Problems: Chronic diseases like heart disease, diabetes, and obesity are more likely to develop as a result of ACEs.

*Mental Health Issues: People with ACEs are more prone to suffer from mental health conditions like post-traumatic stress disorder (PTSD), anxiety, and depression.

Addiction and substance misuse are made more likely by ACEs later in life.

*Poor Academic Performance: ACEs can impair intellectual growth and academic performance, which has an effect on educational attainment.

*Social and Relationship Difficulties: ACE survivors frequently experience difficulty establishing and maintaining healthy relationships, which causes them to feel isolated from others.

*Participation in the Criminal Justice System: ACEs are associated with a higher chance of participating in the criminal justice system, either as offenders or victims.

*Transmission through generations: ACEs can be transmitted down across families, sustaining traumatizing cycles.

ACEs: A Trauma-Informed Approach

Recognizing the long-term impacts of ACEs, a trauma-informed approach aims to address these effects with support and intervention. In order to disrupt the cycle of trauma and encourage healing and resilience, this strategy places a strong emphasis on safety, trust, and empowerment.

Trauma's Reach: How Childhood Trauma Affects Adults' Mental And Physical Health.

Childhood trauma has a lasting effect on both mental and physical health far into adulthood. We shall explore the extensive effects of childhood trauma on adults' well-being in this chapter.

1. Repercussions on mental health:

Adults who endured childhood trauma may develop post-traumatic stress disorder (PTSD), which is characterized by intrusive memories, flashbacks, nightmares, and hypervigilance.

b. Depression and Anxiety: Adult depression and anxiety disorders are more likely to develop in people who experienced childhood trauma. People could deal with ongoing melancholy, pessimism, and excessive concern.

c. Dissociation: As a coping mechanism, dissociation, in which a person separates herself from their thoughts, feelings, or environment, may be experienced by some survivors of childhood trauma.

d. Borderline Personality Disorder (BPD): Childhood trauma is a major risk factor for developing BPD, which can show up as impulsive conduct, unstable relationships, and negative self-image.

e. Substance Abuse: Adults who have experienced childhood trauma may abuse drugs or alcohol to deal with their emotional distress, which can result in substance use disorders.

f. Self-Harm and Suicidal Thoughts: The emotional

agony brought on by childhood trauma may cause people to self-harm or have suicidal thoughts.

2. Effects on Physical Health:

Chronic Health Conditions: Childhood trauma is associated with a higher chance of developing long-term illnesses like diabetes, heart disease, and autoimmune disorders.

b. Modified Stress Response: Trauma can alter the body's stress response system, causing inflammation and persistent stress, both of which are associated with physical health issues.

c. Immune System Suppression: Childhood trauma can impair immunity, leaving people more prone to sickness and infections.

d. Pain Disorders: Chronic pain illnesses like fibromyalgia and migraines are more common in people who have experienced childhood trauma.

3. Relationship and Interpersonal Challenges:

Childhood trauma can interfere with the growth of safe attachment types, making it harder to establish and maintain healthy relationships. a. Attachment Issues.

b. Trust and Intimacy: Adults with a history of childhood trauma frequently struggle with intimacy, trust issues, and a fear of being vulnerable.

Re-victimization: Adults who suffered trauma as children may be more susceptible to experiencing victimization again in both interpersonal and external environments.

4. Maladaptive Behaviors and Coping Mechanisms:

As was already noted, substance misuse can act as an unhelpful coping technique for the emotional suffering brought on by traumatic experiences as a youngster.

b. Eating Disorders: People who struggle to recover control over their lives may develop disorders like anorexia nervosa, bulimia nervosa, and binge-eating disorder.

c. Self-Harm: Some survivors use self-harm to deal with intense emotions and reclaim control over their lives.

d. Avoidance and Isolation: Adults who experienced childhood trauma may withdraw themselves and engage in avoidance practices to safeguard themselves from potential triggers.

5. Obstacles in Reproduction and Parenting:

a. Transmission through generations: Trauma can affect how parents raise their own children, perpetuating the cycle of trauma.

b. Attachment and Parenting Difficulties: Childhood

trauma can make it difficult for an individual to develop strong bonds with their own children and to follow constructive parenting methods.

Giving trauma-informed treatment requires an understanding of the significant and long-lasting impact of childhood trauma on adults' mental and physical health. We will examine tactics and interventions in the chapters that follow in order to lessen these effects and promote recovery and resilience in adult survivors of childhood trauma.

CHAPTER 5: TRAUMA-INFORMED INTERVENTION IN PRACTICE

Assessment And Diagnosis: The Importance Of Accurate Assessment.

An essential first step in trauma-informed care is accurate evaluation since it helps to establish therapies and support that are specifically suited to the patient. This chapter emphasizes the value of rigorous evaluation and the difficulties in detecting conditions connected to trauma.

Why Assessment Is Important

1. Individualized Care: Caregiver and professional understanding of each survivor's particular experiences, requirements, and assets is made possible by accurate evaluation. The foundation for personalised care strategies is this data.

2. Treatment Planning: Assessment informs the creation of effective treatment plans, ensuring that interventions focus on particular issues and symptoms associated to trauma.

3. Recognition of Co-Occurring illnesses: Trauma frequently co-occurs with other mental health illnesses, such as substance use disorders, depression, or anxiety. Effective treatment requires the accurate identification of these comorbidities.

4. Risk assessment: Risk assessment aids in the identification of potential hazards, such as self-harm, suicidal thoughts, or substance addiction, which may call for prompt attention and safety preparation.

5. Monitoring Progress: Through routine evaluation, experts can keep tabs on a survivor's development and alter interventions as necessary to maintain the efficacy of their care.

Trauma Assessment and Diagnosis Challenges

Due to a number of circumstances, assessing trauma-related conditions can be challenging:

1. Underreporting: Trauma victims may conceal their experiences out of embarrassment, fear, or a lack of faith in caretakers. This may cause the

symptoms of trauma to be underreported.

2. Repressed recollections: It may be difficult for certain people to get accurate information because they have repressed or dissociated recollections of traumatic occurrences.

3. Complex Presentations: It can be challenging to diagnose and differentiate trauma survivors because they frequently exhibit a wide variety of symptoms that are similar to those of other mental health illnesses.

4. Cultural considerations: Cultural norms and beliefs might affect how people express and understand their traumatic experiences, necessitating assessment that is sensitive to cultural differences.

5. Developmental Stage: A survivor's developmental stage affects how trauma affects them. Age-appropriate indications of trauma-related symptoms must be taken into account during assessment.

Trauma Assessment Elements

Typically, a thorough trauma assessment consists of:

1. History-taking: Compiling details about the traumatized person's past, such as the types of

incidents, when they happened, how long they lasted, and how frequently.

Examining symptoms including flashbacks, nightmares, hypervigilance, and emotional dysregulation that are linked to trauma.

2. Psychological evaluation: Checking for co-occurring disorders including dissociation, anxiety, or depression.

3. Functional assessment: Analyzing a survivor's daily functioning to spot areas of impairment in areas including job, relationships, and self-care.

4. Performing a safety assessment is the first step in creating safety plans. It involves identifying potential hazards, such as suicidal thoughts, self-harm, or drug usage.

Examining the survivor's strengths, coping skills, and support networks is part of the resilience and strength assessment process.

5. Cultural considerations: Identifying and taking into account cultural elements that may affect how a victim experiences and expresses trauma.

Diagnosis informed by trauma

A trauma-informed approach that takes into account the survivor's experiences and context is necessary for diagnosing trauma-related illnesses. the following common trauma-related diagnoses:

1. Post-Traumatic Stress Disorder (PTSD): Irritating memories, avoidance, detrimental changes in mood or cognition, and increased arousal are the hallmarks of this condition.

2. Dissociative disorders: These may include Depersonalization-Derealization disorder or dissociative identity disorder (DID), which cause changes in consciousness, identity, or perception.

3. Sadness and anxiety disorders: Treatment for sadness and anxiety brought on by trauma frequently involves specialist methods.

4. Attachment Disorders: These conditions can be identified when there has been a disruption in attachment as a result of early trauma.

5. Disorders including substance use: Evaluations should take into account how substance misuse is used as a coping strategy.

Other Specified and Unspecified Trauma-Related Disorders: These diagnoses recognize the variety of ways in which trauma can present itself.

Tools for Trauma-Informed Assessment

The assessment and diagnosis of trauma can

be aided by a number of standardized assessment instruments and questionnaires, such as the Clinician-Administered PTSD Scale (CAPS) or the Adverse Childhood Experiences (ACEs) questionnaire.

The foundation of trauma-informed care is accurate assessment, which provides the crucial data required to customize therapies to each survivor's particular needs and experiences. We shall discuss trauma-informed interventions and treatment approaches informed by careful evaluation in the chapters that follow.

Treatment Modalities: Exploring Various Therapeutic Approaches.

The best treatment technique must be chosen in trauma-informed care in order to meet the special needs of trauma survivors. The many therapeutic modalities and strategies that are successful in fostering healing and recovery are examined in this chapter.

1. Cognitive-Behavioral Therapy (TF-CBT) with a Trauma Focus:

An evidence-based strategy created especially for those who have undergone trauma is called TF-CBT. To address symptoms including flashbacks, nightmares, and avoidance behaviors, it integrates cognitive-behavioral approaches with trauma-specific interventions.

2. EMDR: Eye Movement Desensitization and Reprocessing

EMDR is a therapy method that aids in the processing of traumatic memories and the lessening of the emotional pain they cause in survivors. It entails directed eye movements while thinking back on painful events.

DBT, or dialectical behavior therapy:

Individuals with severe trauma and emotion dysregulation respond well to DBT therapy. It blends mindfulness and acceptance practices with cognitive-behavioral techniques to enhance emotional regulation and interpersonal efficiency.

4. Somatic Experiencing:

SE is concerned with the physiological reactions of the body to trauma. It aids in the physical and mental rehabilitation of survivors by allowing them to release pent-up tension and energy from traumatic experiences.

5. Storytherapy:

By helping survivors create their own unique narratives and reframe their traumatic events, narrative therapy helps them reclaim their feeling of agency and control over their life.

6. Play therapy

When it comes to helping traumatized children, play therapy is particularly beneficial. Children can digest their traumatic experiences and communicate their feelings in non-verbal ways through imaginative play.

7. Art therapy

Through various artistic mediums, survivors can explore their trauma-related feelings and experiences as part of art therapy, which encourages self-expression and insight.

8. Meditation and mindfulness:

Techniques for emotional regulation, stress reduction, and increased self-awareness are all benefits of mindfulness and meditation, which help survivors deal with the symptoms of trauma more effectively.

9. Group Counseling:

Group therapy offers survivors a sympathetic network of people who have gone through similar things. It can ease loneliness and encourage social interaction.

10. Family Counseling:

The effects of trauma on the dynamics and relationships within families are addressed in family therapy. It can aid in enhancing family members' ability to communicate and comprehend one another.

11. Pharmacotherapy

To treat specific trauma-related symptoms including sadness, anxiety, or sleep problems, medication may occasionally be administered. For best results, medication and treatment should be combined.

12. Yoga and movement therapies informed by trauma:

These methods encourage relaxation, bodily awareness, and trauma recovery by fusing physical activity with mindfulness.

13. Therapies that are holistic and complementary:

Acupuncture, massage treatment, and herbal cures are some examples of methods that can support and supplement conventional therapeutic methods.

14. Telehealth and online therapy:

As a result of technological improvements, survivors can now conveniently and remotely get trauma-informed counseling.

Modifying Treatment Approaches:

Various elements, such as the survivor's particular experience, symptomatology, cultural background, and personal preferences, must be taken into consideration while choosing the best therapy option. Effective trauma-informed care frequently combines methods that are adapted to the needs of the client.

We will examine how these therapy methods might be included into trauma-informed care plans in the subsequent chapters, highlighting the significance of a personalised and comprehensive approach to healing and rehabilitation.

Self-Care For Caregivers: Protecting Yourself While Helping Others.

Caregivers and specialists in the field of trauma-informed care are essential in supporting survivors. Caregiving for persons who have suffered trauma, however, may be emotionally and intellectually taxing. This chapter discusses the value of self-care for carers and provides tips for keeping them healthy while providing care.

The Importance of Self-Care for Caregivers

Self-care improves caregivers' resilience, enabling them to better handle the emotional difficulties that come with caring for trauma survivors.

*Quality of Care: Caregivers who put their health first can give survivors better care and support.

*Self-care is a crucial component of preventing burnout, which can result in diminished effectiveness and compassion fatigue.

*Self-care techniques can promote personal and professional growth, enhancing the abilities and empathetic side of caregivers.

Caregiver Self-Care Techniques

*Set Boundaries: To avoid emotional exhaustion and to preserve a good work-life balance, set clear professional boundaries.

*Self-reflection on a regular basis: Monitor your emotional health and, when necessary, seek guidance or help.

*Seek Supervision: Speaking with peers and mentors for advice or supervision can offer helpful direction and a secure setting for discussing difficult cases.

*Self-Care Activities: Make self-care activities a part of your everyday routine. Exercise, meditation, hobbies, and time spent in nature are a few examples.

*Practice mindfulness and relaxation strategies to

manage your stress and keep your emotions in check.

*Maintain Social Connections: Take care of your relationships with friends and family who can offer you emotional support and a feeling of community.

*Professional Development: Invest in your future by going to conferences, workshops, and training sessions on trauma-informed treatment.

*Be nice and sympathetic to oneself by practicing self-compassion. Recognize that working with trauma survivors may cause emotional reactions in you as well.

*Healthy Eating and Sleep: Give healthy eating and getting enough sleep a high priority to promote your physical and emotional wellbeing.

*Consider getting treatment or counseling for yourself if you notice that your job is negatively affecting your emotional well-being.

*Peer Support: Participate in networks or groups that provide peer support so that you can meet people who are in similar caring positions.

*Time management: To avoid extreme stress, effectively manage your time and responsibilities.

How to Spot Compassion Fatigue

Concern over compassion fatigue is a major issue for caregivers who assist trauma survivors. It can show up as physical symptoms, emotional tiredness, and a diminished ability to empathize. For the well-being of caregivers, it is crucial to be aware of the symptoms of compassion fatigue and to take preventative measures to treat them.

Self-care as a Moral Obligation

For caretakers, taking care of oneself is not a luxury but rather a moral obligation. The level of support given to survivors can be compromised when caregivers neglect their own health. Caregiver efficacy, resilience, and commitment to the vital task of trauma-informed care can all be maintained by placing a high priority on self-care.

The practical use of self-care practices for caregivers in diverse trauma-informed care settings and roles will be covered in the future chapters.

CHAPTER 6: HEALING THE WOUNDS

Resilience And Post-Traumatic Growth: How Individuals Can Heal And Grow After Trauma.

A person's capacity for resilience and post-traumatic growth must be understood, even when trauma can result in severe pain and misery. This chapter addresses the ideas of post-traumatic growth and resilience and offers insights into how people might recover and find purpose after going through trauma.

*Resilience: The Ability to Recover from Adversity

The capacity for adaptation and recovery in the face of difficulty, including traumatic situations, is referred to as resilience. It is a dynamic process rather than a set quality that may be developed and made stronger through time.

What Promotes Resilience?

Strong Social Bonds: Strong social connections with friends, family, and communities act as an important protective barrier against the detrimental impacts of trauma.

*Emotional Control: A crucial aspect of resilience is the capacity to control one's emotions and deal with stress.

*Positive Self-Concept: Resilience is influenced by a strong feeling of self-worth and self-efficacy.

*Problem-Solving Skills: Being able to recognize problems and find solutions makes it easier to overcome hardships.

Effective coping techniques, like getting expert assistance or practicing self-care, foster resilience.

*Sense of Purpose: Having a sense of meaning and purpose in life can boost resilience and give people the will to overcome challenges.

Post-Traumatic Development: Recovering Meaning From Trauma

The process of constructive psychological transformation that takes place after trauma is known as post-traumatic growth. It entails both undergoing personal growth and transformation as well as recuperating from the damaging effects of trauma. The following are typical post-traumatic growth domains:

*Interactions: Some people say they have better interactions with others, have more empathy, and have a greater respect for their loved ones.

*Personal Fortitude: Trauma victims frequently find inner reserves of fortitude and resilience they were unaware they possessed.

*Changed Priorities: Trauma can cause people to reconsider their life priorities and pay more attention to the things that are most important to them.

*Greater Appreciation for Life: Survivors could experience an increased awareness of the beauty of life and the present moment.

Spiritual development is the process through which some people enhance their religious or philosophical convictions and feel more a part of something greater than themselves.

Resilience and Post-Traumatic Growth Development

*Seek Professional Support: Therapy or counseling with specialists who are trauma-informed can assist people in processing their experience and creating coping mechanisms.

*Foster Social Connections: Resilience and post-traumatic growth depend on establishing and sustaining supportive relationships.

*Practice mindfulness: Mindfulness methods can assist people in remaining focused on the here and now while managing upsetting thoughts and feelings.

*Prioritize self-care activities that advance your emotional, mental, and physical wellbeing.

*Encourage survivors to reframe their trauma narratives by highlighting their resiliency and strength.

*Create Realistic Goals: In the wake of tragedy, goal-setting can provide one a feeling of direction and purpose.

*Engage in Meaning-Making: Encourage survivors to ponder and derive significance from their experiences, despite hardship.

*Joining support groups with people who have gone through comparable trauma helps promote a sense of community and mutual growth.

Welcome the Journey

Trauma recovery is a nonlinear process that differs from person to person. While some people may recover from trauma and experience post-traumatic growth quite rapidly, others could need more time. It is crucial to approach this path with tolerance, compassion for oneself, and an open heart, understanding that growth and healing are possible even in the midst of the most difficult circumstances.

Trauma Processing: Techniques For Processing Traumatic Memories.

An essential first step in trauma rehabilitation is processing distressing memories. Unprocessed trauma can result in a variety of uncomfortable symptoms, and trauma survivors frequently carry the emotional burden of their experiences with them. This chapter will look at methods and strategies for handling traumatic memories in a trauma-informed care framework.

Understanding the processing of trauma

In order to assist survivors make sense of their experiences, lessen emotional suffering, and advance recovery, trauma processing entails the methodical and therapeutic study of traumatic memories. Memories of trauma can be processed to:

Integration is the process of weaving together

jumbled or disjointed memories into a seamless story.

*Emotional Control: Assisting survivors in controlling intense feelings brought on by painful memories.

*Reducing Symptoms: Lessening trauma-related symptoms include nightmares, hypervigilance, and flashbacks.

Regaining control over one's life and story is known as "reclaiming control."

Techniques for Processing Trauma

1. Therapeutic Narrative Exposure (NET):

NET entails writing a thorough chronological account of the survivor's life that includes all traumatic experiences. This story aids survivors in processing and placing their experiences in context.

2. Therapy for Prolonged Exposure (PE):

PE emphasizes controlled exposure to gradually confront and process traumatic memories. The emotional anguish brought on by traumatic memories is lessened because to this desensitization process.

3. Therapy for cognitive processing (CPT):

CPT assists trauma survivors in questioning and reframing unhelpful attitudes and beliefs about their trauma. This mental remodeling encourages a more impartial viewpoint.

4. Emotional Memory Desensitization and Reprocessing, or EMDR

While processing traumatic memories, EMDR uses bilateral stimulation such as guided eye movements. This method aids in the reprocessing of upsetting memories and helps survivors feel less emotionally charged.

5. Expressive therapies and the arts:

Survivors can process and communicate their traumatic experiences in other ways by using creative mediums like writing, music, and painting.

6. Experiencing Somatically (SE):

SE is concerned with the physiological reactions of the body to trauma. Through gentle body-based exercises, it aids in the release of tension and repressed trauma energy in survivors.

Approaches Based on Mindfulness:

When processing traumatic memories, survivors can use mindfulness practices to keep their feet firmly planted in the present. These methods support self-compassion and impartiality.

Structured Journaling and Writing:

Survivors can process and make sense of their traumatic experiences in a systematic fashion with the aid of guided writing exercises and journaling.

The Construction of a Safe Processing Container

It might be emotionally difficult to process painful memories, which may cause momentary distress. When utilizing trauma processing procedures, a secure and encouraging therapy atmosphere is crucial. Important ideas include:

Before beginning trauma processing, make sure survivors feel safe and believe in the therapist or facilitator.

*Emotional Regulation: In order to control distress while processing, teach survivors grounding and emotion-regulation strategies.

*Choice and Control: Give trauma survivors the freedom to choose when and how to process their experiences. Don't put pressure on them.

*Continuous Assessment: Keep track of survivors' emotional health at all times and modify interventions as necessary.

*Encourage survivors to incorporate their experiences with processing into a larger story of healing and recovery.

Stress the importance of survivors using self-care techniques both before and after trauma processing sessions.

Processing Trauma as a Journey

Trauma processing is a journey that takes place over time rather than being a single occurrence. As they continue to heal, survivors may return and process horrific memories. Techniques and methods for processing trauma should be adapted to the individual's needs and rate of processing.

The practical uses of trauma processing approaches in diverse contexts and settings for trauma-informed care will be covered in the chapters that follow.

Building Resilience: Strengthening The Inner Resources Of Trauma Survivors.

Resilience is a powerful inner quality that enables individuals to bounce back from adversity and build a fulfilling life after trauma. This chapter explores the principles and strategies for building resilience in trauma survivors, helping them harness their inner resources to overcome the challenges they face.

Understanding Resilience

Resilience is not a fixed trait; rather, it is a dynamic process that can be cultivated and strengthened over time. It involves the ability to adapt to stress, recover from setbacks, and emerge from adversity with newfound strength and wisdom. Resilience empowers trauma survivors to regain control over their lives and navigate the path to healing.

The Components of Resilience

Resilience comprises several key components that contribute to a survivor's ability to overcome trauma:

*Emotional Regulation: The capacity to recognize, manage, and cope with difficult emotions is central to resilience. Survivors learn to express their feelings constructively and avoid being overwhelmed by them.

*Positive Self-Concept: A healthy self-esteem and self-worth provide a strong foundation for resilience. Trauma survivors who value themselves are better equipped to face challenges and setbacks.

*Social Support: Strong social connections, whether with friends, family, or a supportive community, serve as a vital resource during difficult times. Social support enhances resilience by providing emotional and practical assistance.

*Problem-Solving Skills: Resilient individuals possess effective problem-solving skills that enable them to navigate challenges and setbacks constructively. They approach problems with a sense of agency and confidence.

*Coping Strategies: Resilience is bolstered by adaptive coping strategies. Survivors learn to cope with adversity by developing healthy mechanisms for dealing with stress, such as mindfulness, relaxation, or seeking professional support.

Strategies for Building Resilience

*Therapeutic Support: Engage in trauma-focused therapy or counseling with a trauma-informed professional who can provide guidance, emotional support, and tools for building resilience.

*Emotional Awareness: Encourage survivors to develop emotional awareness and literacy, helping them recognize and express their feelings in a healthy manner.

*Mindfulness and Self-Care: Teach survivors mindfulness techniques and self-care practices to manage stress, stay present, and nurture their well-being.

*Positive Affirmations: Encourage survivors to practice positive self-talk and affirmations to boost self-esteem and self-worth.

*Problem-Solving Skills: Assist survivors in developing effective problem-solving skills by breaking down challenges into manageable steps and brainstorming solutions.

*Social Connection: Facilitate opportunities for survivors to build and maintain meaningful social connections, which serve as a critical source of support.

*Community Involvement: Engaging in community activities or volunteering can provide survivors with a sense of purpose and belonging.

*Strengths-Based Approach: Focus on survivors' strengths and abilities rather than their vulnerabilities. This strengths-based approach can bolster their self-confidence.

*Resilience-Building Workshops: Offer workshops or group sessions specifically designed to enhance resilience through skill-building and peer support.

*Encourage Growth Mindset: Foster a growth mindset, emphasizing that challenges can be opportunities for growth and learning.

*Setting Realistic Goals: Help survivors set achievable goals and celebrate their successes, no matter how small.

Resilience as a Lifelong Journey

Building resilience is an ongoing and lifelong journey. Trauma survivors may encounter setbacks, but with the right support and strategies, they can continue to grow and adapt. Resilience empowers survivors to not only recover from trauma but also to thrive and lead fulfilling lives.

In the subsequent chapters, we will explore practical applications of resilience-building strategies within various trauma-informed care settings and contexts.

CHAPTER 7: EMPOWERING THE SURVIVOR

Empowerment And Recovery: Fostering Self-Determination And Autonomy.

In trauma-informed treatment, empowerment and recovery are linked ideas. This chapter examines how empowering trauma survivors and supporting their autonomy and self-determination might speed up their road to recovery and healing.

Power: Taking Back Control

The process of empowering people to take charge of their life, make decisions, and stand up for their needs and rights. Empowerment for trauma survivors entails restoring a sense of agency and control that their traumatic experiences may have taken away.

The Value of Empowerment in the Recovery Process

For a number of reasons, empowerment is a crucial principle in trauma-informed care.

*Regaining Agency: Trauma survivors may have a sense of helplessness and helplessness. Survivors who feel empowered reclaim control over their lives.

*Building Self-Esteem: Empowerment increases one's sense of self-worth and self-esteem, allowing survivors to see themselves as competent, worthwhile people.

*Self-Advocacy Promotion: Survivors who feel empowered are more likely to speak up for themselves both inside and outside of the therapeutic alliance.

*Enhancing Resilience: Resilience is cultivated by an empowered attitude, which enables survivors to tackle adversity with tenacity and assurance.

Methods for Promoting Empowerment

Encourage survivors to actively participate in decisions regarding their care and treatment by giving them the freedom to select the options that feel appropriate to them.

*Education and knowledge: Enable survivors to make informed decisions by arming them with thorough knowledge about trauma, available treatments, and other resources.

*Strengths-Based Approach: Instead than concentrating just on survivors' vulnerabilities, highlight survivors' strengths, abilities, and skills.

*Goal-setting: Work with survivors to establish attainable objectives that reflect their beliefs and aspirations.

*Teaching survivors how to state their demands, create boundaries, and interact with healthcare professionals and support networks are examples of self-advocacy skills.

*Crisis planning: Give survivors a sense of control during trying times by including them in the creation of crisis plans.

*Create a supportive setting so survivors can feel heard, accepted, and respected. This environment should promote empowerment.

A Personal Journey in Recovery

There is no one method that works for everyone to recover from trauma because it is such a highly personal experience. Finding a future that fits the survivor's aims and values rather than deleting the past is the purpose of recovery.

The Levels of Recuperation

Usually, recovery happens in stages:

*Stabilization and Safety: Providing stability and immediate safety for the survivor.

*Addressing and processing painful memories and feelings are important steps in the healing process.

*Growth and Integration: Regaining a sense of self and integrating the healing experiences.

*Community Reintegration: Getting back in touch with the local area, building up a network of helpful contacts, and reclaiming a purposeful existence.

Independence in Recovery

The path to healing is intertwined with empowerment:

*Encourage survivors to actively participate in the development of safety plans and initiatives.

*Encourage survivors to select treatment modalities that speak to them and are consistent with their objectives for healing.

*Self-Advocacy: Empower survivors to speak up for themselves in therapeutic settings and in everyday situations.

*Goal-setting: Work with survivors to establish recovery objectives that are in line with their principles and ambitions.

*Self-Discovery: As they begin to reconstruct their life, assist survivors in identifying their strengths, passions, and interests.

*Peer Support: Introduce survivors to networks and peer support groups that give them confidence through their common experiences.

*Encouragement of community involvement can help survivors create a network of support that will aid in their recovery.

Recovery as a Process, Not a Goal

The process of recovery is nonlinear and continuing. It involves obstacles, difficulties, and development. It is possible for survivors to manage these complications and embrace the potential of a meaningful and rewarding life beyond trauma by encouraging empowerment and autonomy within the rehabilitation process.

Building A Supportive Community: The Role Of Family, Friends, And Community In Recovery.

Trauma recovery is a road that is frequently impossible to take by oneself. In this chapter, we examine the critical function that friends, family, and the larger community play in fostering the healing of trauma survivors.

The Importance of Complementary Relationships

For trauma survivors to heal and rehabilitate, supportive relationships are essential. These connections offer the emotional security, affirmation, and sense of community that are crucial for a survivor's progress and well-being.

*Friend and family assistance

Family and friends can offer a secure place for survivors to share their sentiments without fear of rejection.

*Validation: When loved ones affirm a survivor's experiences and feelings, it lessens their sense of loneliness and self-doubt.

*Family and friends can provide survivors with practical assistance, such as assistance with daily duties, transportation, or childcare, which can reduce stress and enable survivors to concentrate on their rehabilitation.

*Loved ones can act as survivors' advocates by guiding them through the healthcare system and connecting them to the resources they need.

Consistency: A reliable and stable support system offers predictability, which is essential for survivors' feelings of security.

The Community's Function

Support from the community goes beyond a person's close friends and family. It includes broader community networks, institutions, and programs that can aid a survivor's road to recovery:

*Support Groups: People who have undergone similar trauma can connect with one another in support groups and feel a feeling of belonging. They provide a secure setting for assistance and sharing.

*Accessible mental health resources in the neighborhood are necessary for survivors to receive medical attention and therapy.

*Employment and education resources in the community can aid in giving survivors a renewed sense of direction and stability in their life.

*Crisis Helplines: In times of crisis, crisis helplines and hotlines can provide instant aid.

*Community Programs: Programs that are centered on health, the arts, physical fitness, or other hobbies can assist survivors in connecting with their neighborhood and reclaiming their identity.

*Organizations in the community that prioritize providing trauma-informed treatment foster a welcoming environment for survivors seeking help.

Creating a Community of Support

*Education: Spread awareness of trauma and its repercussions among family members, friends, and the general public. This can promote understanding and lessen stigma.

*Encourage survivors and their support systems to communicate honestly and openly. Clarifying expectations, needs, and boundaries through communication.

*Respect the interests and boundaries of survivors. It's crucial to know when to give assistance and when to give space.

*Self-Care: Promote self-care through social networks. Taking care of oneself makes it easier for loved ones to support the survivor.

*Engage with neighborhood groups and resources that place a high priority on trauma-informed care.

Promote more accessibility and awareness.

*Actively and without bias listen to survivors. The most important type of support might occasionally be as simple as being aware and present.

Assisting friends and family

It's important to recognize that helping a trauma survivor can be emotionally taxing for friends and family. For those offering help, self-care, education, and access to support are crucial.

Building Resilience and Healing

In order to create a supportive atmosphere, it is important to create a setting that encourages recovery and resilience as well as meeting immediate needs. Communities may be effective agents of healing by working together to understand, empathize with, and commit to the needs of trauma survivors.

The practical methods for establishing and maintaining supportive communities in the context of trauma-informed care will be discussed in the chapters that follow.

Advocacy And Social Change: How Trauma

Survivors Can Become Advocates For Change.

Trauma survivors have a distinct viewpoint and firsthand experience that can inspire effective advocacy campaigns and advance larger social change. This chapter examines the ways in which survivors can act as advocates, spreading knowledge, influencing legislation, and promoting a society that is better informed about trauma.

Survivor Advocacy's Power

Trauma survivors frequently have a firsthand knowledge of the difficulties, limitations, and service gaps that exist in society. This realization can be used to create significant change on multiple levels:

*Awareness-Raising: Survivor advocates can use their personal experiences to spread the word about the prevalence and effects of trauma. Personal accounts can make the problem more relatable and less stigmatizing.

*Policy Influence: In order to make sure that policies relating to support services, mental health, and trauma are more attentive to the needs of survivors, survivors' advocates can seek to change and influence these policies.

*Promoting treatments: Survivor advocates can promote better accessibility to crisis intervention, trauma-informed mental health treatments, and support networks.

*Education and Training: A focus of survivor advocacy might include advancing trauma-informed education and training within institutions, institutions of higher learning, and communities.

Survival Advocacy Techniques

The art of storytelling may be a potent tool for connecting with others and spreading awareness. Advocates for survivors should be ready to do so in a way that is both safe and considerate of their own wellbeing.

*Peer Support: Establishing peer support networks and advocacy organizations can give survivors a forum for collaboration and voice amplification.

*Partnerships: Working together with already-existing advocacy groups, mental health professionals, and neighborhood organizations can help survivor advocates maximize their efforts.

*Education and Training: To hone their advocacy abilities and have a better understanding of the issues, survivor advocates can take part in training sessions and workshops.

*Advocate for trauma-informed policies and financing with politicians and policymakers. This is a crucial step in bringing about systemic change.

*Media Engagement: Using media outlets to reach a larger audience, such as producing articles, doing interviews, or using social media, can benefit survivors' rights advocates.

Self-Care for Advocates for Survivors

As it frequently entails revisiting and discussing terrible memories, survivor advocacy can be emotionally draining. Survivor advocates must practice self-care and seek for support:

*Peer Support: Make connections with other survivors' rights activists for understanding and support.

*Therapy and counseling: Use these services to process your feelings and cope with the emotional strain of your advocacy activity.

*Set boundaries around your lobbying efforts to safeguard your mental wellbeing.

*Prioritize self-care activities like mindfulness, exercise, and rest to keep your equilibrium.

Making Change That Is Trauma-Informed

In addition to increasing awareness, survivor advocacy helps build a society that is more sensitive to the needs of survivors and informed about trauma. Survivor advocates are crucial in lowering the occurrence of trauma and enhancing the resources accessible to individuals who have experienced it by pushing for change at the individual, community, and institutional levels.

Within trauma-informed treatment settings and larger societal contexts, we will discuss practical options for survivor advocacy and social change in the upcoming chapters.

CHAPTER 8: TRAUMA-INFORMED CARE IN DIVERSE CONTEXTS

Trauma In Schools: Creating Trauma-Informed Classrooms And Educational Environments.

Schools are important in the lives of kids and teens, especially those who have been through trauma. This chapter examines the significance of developing classrooms and learning settings that are trauma-informed in order to promote the academic, emotional, and social wellbeing of students who have experienced trauma.

Understanding the Effects of Trauma in Schools

Trauma can have a substantial impact on a student's capacity to learn and succeed in a classroom. Traumatic events in schools can have the following effects:

Academic issues: Trauma can affect a student's ability to focus, remember things, and think clearly, which can cause issues in the classroom.

Students may display issues with their conduct, such as acting out, defiance, withdrawal, or hostility.

Trauma can result in emotional distress, which can induce symptoms of anxiety, sadness, and post-traumatic stress disorder.

Students that struggle socially may find it difficult to communicate with others, build positive relationships, or take part in class activities.

Making Schools Trauma-Informed

Learning about how trauma affects behavior and learning is a hallmark of trauma-informed classrooms. In these settings, educators place a high priority on the students' emotional health and safety. The following are some methods for developing trauma-informed classrooms:

Training for Educators: Give teachers instruction on trauma awareness, its effects, and trauma-informed teaching techniques.

Create a physically and emotionally safe environment in the classroom where students will feel respected and cherished.

Establish clear and consistent classroom expectations and practices to help students feel less anxious.

Teach kids how to control their emotions in order to cope with stress and unpleasant feelings.

Strengths-based approach: Highlight student accomplishments and strengths to raise their self-esteem and confidence.

Flexibility: Adapt your teaching methods as needed to meet the needs of your students.

Include mindfulness activities and relaxation methods in your classroom to help students stay present and manage stress.

Empathy and Understanding: Encourage educators to have empathy and understanding for the emotional needs of their students.

Supporting Policies That Consider Trauma

Institutions of higher learning can implement procedures and policies that encourage trauma-informed methods:

Anti-Bullying Programs: Implement anti-bullying initiatives to establish inclusive and secure learning environments in schools.

Mental Health Services: Ensure that students who have experienced trauma have access to counseling and other mental health services in their schools.

Reduce interpersonal disputes by teaching pupils effective communication and conflict resolution techniques.

Community Partnerships: Work together with neighborhood organizations to give students and families more resources and support.

Engagement of Parents and Caregivers: Include parents and caregivers in the educational process and give them resources to support the emotional wellbeing of their children.

Integrated Support Teams

A thorough strategy for addressing trauma-related difficulties can be achieved by establishing multidisciplinary support teams inside schools:

School counselors: Students who have experienced trauma may get individual and group counseling from school counselors.

School psychologists: Psychologists can carry out evaluations, create intervention strategies, and offer extra assistance to pupils with complicated needs.

Work together with special education services to make sure that students who are experiencing learning difficulties as a result of trauma are given the proper accommodations.

Work with community partners to link students and families with additional support, such as social services and mental health organizations.

Support for Schools that are Trauma-Informed

The following are some ways that parents, guardians, and teachers can promote trauma-informed practices in their schools:

Educate the community, parents, and school personnel about the value of trauma-informed instruction through awareness campaigns.

Advocate for trauma-informed policies and procedures at the state and school district levels through policy advocacy.

Parent Education: Offer materials and workshops to help parents comprehend the effects of trauma and how to support their children.

Conclusion

For students who have experienced trauma, establishing trauma-informed classrooms and learning environments is a crucial first step in promoting their academic, emotional, and social wellbeing. Educators and school communities may create a more welcoming and supportive learning environment for all kids by identifying the special needs of these individuals and putting trauma-informed strategies into practice.

Trauma In Healthcare: Integrating Trauma-Informed Care Into Medical Settings.

Trauma survivors frequently seek physical and mental healing in healthcare settings, such as hospitals, clinics, and medical offices. In order to support patients who have suffered trauma and enhance general healthcare outcomes, this chapter examines the significance of incorporating trauma-informed care into healthcare contexts.

Trauma's Effect on Healthcare

The impact of trauma on a person's physical and mental health can be profound. It is crucial for healthcare providers to comprehend these effects:

Physical Health: Trauma can be a factor in the development of chronic illnesses like heart disease, autoimmune diseases, and pain disorders.

Mental Health: Trauma survivors may struggle with mental health issues such depression, anxiety, PTSD, and substance misuse.

Healthcare Use: Trauma survivors may use healthcare services more frequently because of physical and mental health problems that are linked to trauma.

Communication Issues: Trauma can make it difficult for a patient to adequately express their symptoms, medical history, and treatment preferences.

The fundamentals of trauma-informed care

Safety: Establish a psychologically and physically secure healthcare setting where patients feel respected and at ease.

Transparency and Trustworthiness: Promote trust by being open and honest with patients, including by outlining treatment alternatives and including them in decision-making.

Peer Support: Provide mentoring and peer support initiatives that pair patients with people who have gone through comparable trauma.

To provide comprehensive care, promote cooperation between medical professionals, mental health specialists, and social workers.

Empowering patients through their participation in healthcare decisions and respect for their autonomy.

Cultural Sensitivity: Recognize and respond to the various cultural backgrounds and experiences of your patients.

Trauma screening

One crucial step in identifying patients who can benefit from trauma-informed therapy is routinely screening for a history of trauma:

Implement universal screening for traumatic experience during intake assessments in healthcare facilities.

Use non-intrusive, trauma-informed questioning methods that are considerate of your patients' emotional needs.

Ensuring patient confidentiality and privacy during trauma screening talks.

Communication That Is Trauma-Informed

The foundation of trauma-informed care in healthcare settings is effective communication:

Active listening should be used to make patients feel validated and heard.

Empathetic Reactions: Show empathy for the patients' emotional discomfort and refrain from using critical or dismissive remarks.

Use language that is trauma-informed to prevent upsetting or retraumatizing patients.

Trauma Narratives: If patients wish to do so, they should be given the freedom to do so at their own pace.

Intervention in crises and de-escalation

To properly respond to patients in distress, healthcare professionals should be trained in crisis intervention and de-escalation techniques:

De-escalation Training: Educate patients on how to diffuse difficult situations and lessen their anxiety.

Establish specialist crisis intervention teams within healthcare facilities to assist people who are in immediate trouble.

Cross-disciplinary Cooperation

In order to deliver trauma-informed healthcare, interdisciplinary teamwork between healthcare professionals, mental health experts, social workers, and support staff is essential:

Encourage team-based care that takes both the requirements of physical and mental health into account.

Consultation and Referral: Ensure that when required, trauma-informed consultation and referral resources are available to healthcare professionals.

Healthcare Providers' Self-Care

Healthcare professionals may experience emotional strain when working with trauma survivors. Support and self-care are crucial for their wellbeing:

Provide opportunities for debriefing and consultation, as well as supervision and support for healthcare professionals.

Encourage healthcare professionals to exercise self-care in order to manage stress and avoid burnout.

Conclusion

For healthcare systems to effectively address the physical and emotional needs of trauma survivors, trauma-informed care must be included. Healthcare institutions may establish environments that support healing, resilience, and better healthcare outcomes for trauma survivors by adopting trauma-informed principles, screening for trauma history, improving communication, and fostering interdisciplinary collaboration.

Trauma In Criminal Justice: Transforming The Justice System Through Trauma-Informed Practices.

Many victims of trauma have interactions with the criminal justice system in their daily lives. The need for and advantages of incorporating trauma-informed methods into the criminal justice system —which includes law enforcement, the courts, and correctional facilities—are examined in this chapter.

Recognizing Trauma in the Criminal Justice System

People who work in the criminal justice system may experience trauma in their lives, including:

Victims: Many people who are victimized by crime go through trauma as a result of being hurt.

Offenders: Trauma histories are common among those who interact with the criminal justice system and might influence criminal behavior.

Professionals in the justice system: Due to their line of work, law enforcement officers, judges, attorneys, and correctional staff may also be exposed to secondary trauma or suffer from vicarious trauma.

Trauma and Its Effects on the Criminal Justice System

Re-victimization: As they negotiate a system that might not be trauma-informed, trauma survivors inside the court system may experience re-victimization.

Recidivism: Without addressing the underlying causes of their criminal behavior, offenders with traumatic past may be more likely to reoffend.

Justice professionals may endure secondary trauma, which could affect their ability to do their jobs and general well-being.

Criminal Justice Practices That Consider Trauma

Training and Education: Educate justice professionals on trauma-informed concepts and practices, particularly how to recognize and comprehend the effects of trauma.

Utilize trauma-informed screening and assessment techniques to identify people with traumatic backgrounds and determine their needs.

Communication: Provide training in trauma-informed communication methods to those working in the legal system, with a focus on active listening, empathy, and sensitivity.

Utilize trauma-informed police techniques to defuse situations and lessen the need for force.

Adopt trauma-informed courtroom procedures that take trauma survivors' needs and triggers into account while hearing cases.

Rehabilitation Programs: Create reentry and rehabilitation plans for offenders that take trauma into account and address any underlying trauma that may have influenced their criminal behavior.

In order to respond to people in crisis with empathy and the proper de-escalation strategies, law enforcement authorities should establish specialist crisis intervention teams.

Working together across systems

Foster interagency cooperation between the criminal justice system, social services, mental health services, and community organizations to provide complete support for trauma victims.

Transform correctional facilities into trauma-informed settings with a focus on rehabilitation rather than punishment. Trauma-Informed Jails and Prisons.

Investigate restorative justice strategies that place a focus on forgiveness and responsibility for both victims and offenders.

assisting legal professionals

Self-Care: To lessen the effects of secondary trauma, promote self-care behaviors and mental health support for justice professionals.

Peer Support: To offer emotional support and to share coping mechanisms, create peer support networks inside justice organizations.

Support for Community Reintegration

Create trauma-informed reentry programs that offer resources and assistance to people returning to society following incarceration.

Community-Based resources: Introduce people to trauma-informed community resources, such as housing, employment assistance, and mental health care.

Conclusion

For the criminal justice system to effectively meet the multifaceted needs of people who have suffered trauma, whether as victims or offenders, it is imperative to integrate trauma-informed methods. The justice system may move toward a more compassionate and successful approach that promotes healing and lowers recidivism by recognizing the impact of trauma, offering training and education, and encouraging interagency collaboration.

CHAPTER 9: ETHICAL CONSIDERATIONS IN TRAUMA-INFORMED INTERVENTION

Confidentiality And Boundaries: Navigating The Ethical Dilemmas Of Trauma Care.

Complex ethical considerations must be made while providing trauma-informed care, particularly with regard to boundaries and confidentiality. The ethical issues that practitioners providing trauma care must overcome are examined in this chapter, along with advice on how to do so while adhering to the fundamentals of trauma-informed practice.

the significance of discretion

Building trust with trauma survivors requires confidentiality, which is a cornerstone of the therapeutic partnership. It entails protecting the confidentiality and security of the personal data that clients disclose while receiving treatment and support services.

Ethics of Confidentiality Issues

Mandatory Reporting: In some states, medical personnel are required by law to alert authorities when specific types of trauma, such as child abuse or the threat of serious harm to oneself or others, occur. The desire for privacy of a survivor could be at odds with this commitment.

Informed consent: From the beginning of therapy, trauma survivors should be thoroughly informed about the boundaries of confidentiality. It can be hard to strike a balance between the necessity of transparency and a survivor's degree of comfort.

Confidentiality with Minors: When working with young people who have experienced trauma, professionals must strike a difficult balance between protecting the privacy of the minor and involving parents or other legal guardians as necessary.

Group therapy participants may share private information with one another in a confidential context. It might be difficult to protect individual privacy while promoting group cohesiveness.

Managing Ethical Conundrums

Obtain survivors' informed consent by keeping them informed about the boundaries of confidentiality, including required reporting requirements. Make sure that survivors provide consent after being fully informed.

Legal Responsibilities: Become familiar with local laws and ordinances pertaining to obligatory reporting and confidentiality. Be ready to advise surviving family members of your legal obligations.

Balancing Safety: When moral conundrums present themselves, put safety first. If there are worries that the survivor or others will be harmed, you should report the situation and take action in accordance with established legal and ethical guidelines.

When faced with challenging ethical decisions, seek supervision and advice from knowledgeable experts or ethics committees. Peer case discussion can offer insightful advice and helpful insights.

Set boundaries based on trauma

In order to provide trauma-informed treatment, boundaries must be set up clearly and appropriately. Because trauma victims may have experienced boundary violations, it's crucial to set up good examples of boundaries in therapy settings.

Understand the distinction between boundary crossings and violations, which are damaging breaches of professional boundaries as opposed to flexible reactions within professional positions. Try to stay away from the latter.

Self-Disclosure: Use self-disclosure as a therapeutic strategy with caution. While it can occasionally be beneficial to share personal experiences, it should always be done carefully and with the survivor's best interests in mind.

Recognize and deal with transference and countertransference, which are the therapist's emotional responses to the survivor and the unconscious redirection of sentiments toward them, respectively. In addressing these dynamics, supervision can be extremely helpful.

Dual relationships, in which the therapist plays multiple roles with the survivor (such as therapist and friend or therapist and employer), should be avoided since they can damage impartiality and professional limits.

Conclusion

A challenging but crucial part of offering trauma-informed treatments is striking a balance between the ethical concerns of confidentiality and limits in trauma care. Professionals can manage these moral conundrums while honoring the principles of trauma-informed treatment by remaining transparent, seeking supervision and advice when necessary, and placing the survivor's safety and well-being first.

Cultural Competence: Addressing Trauma Within Diverse Cultural Contexts.

Trauma is a common human experience, yet how it manifests, is perceived, and what effect it has varies across many cultural contexts. This chapter discusses the value of cultural competence in trauma-informed care and provides advice on how to effectively handle trauma in communities with a variety of cultural traditions.

Culture Competence and Its Importance

Understanding, respecting, and effectively addressing the cultural requirements and preferences of individuals and groups are all aspects of cultural competence. Cultural competence is essential in trauma-informed care for a number of reasons:

Cultural Variations in Trauma Response: Due

to varying cultural norms, beliefs, and coping mechanisms, trauma can show itself in various cultural groups in different ways.

Barriers to Care: A lack of cultural competence can cause misunderstandings, mistrust, and difficulties for people from different backgrounds in receiving trauma-informed care.

Respecting Diverse viewpoints: Cultural competency recognizes and values the various viewpoints that exist on trauma, enabling professionals to adapt their methods to meet the needs of both individuals and communities.

Recommendations for Culturally Appropriate Trauma Care

Adopt a position of cultural humility by admitting that you might not fully comprehend or be an authority on every culture. Approach each person with curiosity and an open mind.

Conduct cultural evaluations to comprehend the person's cultural background, values, and viewpoints on trauma and recovery.

Be mindful to cultural conventions and practices, especially when it comes to touch, eye contact, and communication patterns, which can differ greatly among countries.

Language and communication: When there are language issues, make sure that there is good communication by offering interpreters or multilingual workers. Avoid jargon and speak plainly.

Respect for Healing Rituals: When suitable and desired by the patient, respect and incorporate traditional healing rituals into trauma-informed care.

Trauma Narrative: Be aware that there may be cultural differences in how trauma narratives are seen, and that some people may be unwilling to discuss traumatic events because of cultural taboos or stigmas.

Collaboration with Cultural Experts: When dealing with people from particular cultural communities, collaborate with cultural experts, local leaders, or elders.

Avoid Stereotyping: Refrain from assuming things about people or applying stereotypes to them based on their cultural background. Recognize the individuality of every person.

Competence in Trauma-Informed Culture

Understanding Trauma Across Cultures: Become

knowledgeable about the cultural manifestations of trauma, including the symptoms, reactions, and healing techniques that are unique to each culture.

Participate in trauma training programs that include cultural competency components, as these will provide you the tools and techniques you need to treat trauma in a variety of cultural situations.

Examine your organization's trauma-informed services for cultural sensitivity and make any required modifications to better serve a varied clientele.

Promote policies that encourage cultural competence and diversity in trauma-informed care systems by speaking out in favor of cultural competency in policy.

input and Adaptation: Encourage input from clients from a range of cultural backgrounds, then make the necessary adjustments to your trauma-informed procedures.

Community Participation

A crucial component of cultural competence in trauma-informed care is interaction with diverse cultural communities:

Partnerships with the Community: Work together

with community groups and leaders to foster a climate of trust and to promote the provision of trauma-informed treatment within diverse cultural contexts.

Participate in or organize cultural awareness events to promote communication and understanding between trauma specialists and other cultural groups.

Conclusion

In order to ensure that people from different cultural backgrounds receive effective and culturally sensitive care, cultural competence is a crucial component of trauma-informed care. Professionals can deliver trauma care that is truly responsive to the particular needs and views of each individual and community by acknowledging and respecting cultural diversity.

Trauma And Intersectionality: Recognizing How Multiple Identities Intersect With Trauma.

Trauma is not something that people experience in a vacuum; it interacts with many facets of one's identity, including ethnicity, gender, sexual orientation, handicap, and socioeconomic class. This chapter explores the idea of intersectionality in trauma-informed care, highlighting the significance of identifying and resolving the particular difficulties faced by people who have many intersecting identities.

Intersectionality: An Understanding

The term "intersectionality," coined by Kimberlé Crenshaw, recognizes how several social identities, such as race, gender, class, sexual orientation, and ability, intersect and interact to influence one's experiences and vulnerabilities. Intersectionality aids professionals in understanding that trauma is not a universal experience and that people who identify with many marginalized identities face particular difficulties in receiving trauma-informed care.

Intersectionality's Effect on Trauma

Cumulative Oppression: People who have many marginalized identities may experience cumulative oppression, when trauma and prejudice interact and both have a greater negative effect.

Accessibility Issues: Intersectional identities can produce special accessibility issues, such as distrust of institutions, prejudice in the medical field, and cultural insensitivity.

Complex trauma reactions: For people with intersecting identities, trauma reactions may be complicated and exacerbated, making it difficult to recognize and meet their needs.

Isolation and Stigma: People may feel isolated and reluctant to seek care as a result of the stigma attached to both trauma and marginalized identities.

Intersectional Trauma-Informed Care Principles

Cultural humility means approaching each person with an understanding that their experiences are impacted by the overlapping of several identities.

Cultural competency: To better comprehend the struggles and experiences faced by those with intersecting identities, invest in ongoing cultural competency training.

Adopt an anti-oppression paradigm that actively seeks to recognize and address the underlying injustices that cause trauma.

When creating trauma-informed programs and policies, it is important to consider a variety of viewpoints and views in order to make sure that all people's needs are met.

Provide trauma-informed care that is culturally

adapted and takes into account each person's unique cultural, racial, and gender identities.

Advocacy and Empowerment: Encourage people with multiple intersecting identities to stand up for their rights and the rights of their communities by giving them the tools they need to do so.

Opportunities and Challenges

evaluation: Create evaluation procedures and tools that take into account the particular experiences of people who have numerous intersecting identities.

Research and Data: Promote studies on the intersectionality of trauma to learn more about how trauma affects different communities and how they respond to it.

Training and education: Include intersectional viewpoints in trauma professional training programs.

Policy and Advocacy: Promote policies and practices that, within trauma-informed care systems, specifically address the needs of people with intersecting identities.

Community Participation

Partnerships: Work together to develop welcoming and all-inclusive trauma-informed care systems with community groups and leaders who serve populations impacted by overlapping identities.

Promote diversity, equity, and inclusion in recruiting, policies, and practices to foster cultural competence inside organizations.

Conclusion

A crucial perspective for understanding trauma and trauma-informed care is intersectionality. Professionals can offer more fair and effective support, ensuring that no one is left behind in the process of healing and recovery, by taking into account the particular difficulties and experiences that people with many intersecting identities face.

CHAPTER 10:
LOOKING FORWARD

The Future Of Trauma-Informed Care: Emerging Trends And Research.

In understanding and addressing the effects of trauma on individuals and communities, trauma-informed treatment has gone a long way. This chapter examines future avenues for research, new trends, and the possibility for trauma-informed care.

Using technology in combination

Telehealth & Teletherapy: As telehealth platforms are used more frequently, those who live in rural or underserved locations will have easier access to trauma therapy and support services.

Digital mental health apps: The creation and adoption of platforms and apps for digital mental health that apply trauma-informed concepts will increase.

Virtual Reality Therapy: For the treatment of trauma and exposure therapy, virtual reality therapy may be used more frequently.

Developments in Neuroscience

Neurofeedback: New developments in neurofeedback approaches may offer more accurate and efficient ways to control the brain's reaction to trauma.

Pharmacological interventions: Studies investigating the use of medications to treat trauma-related illnesses like PTSD may result in more specialized and individualized therapies.

Intersectional and Cultural Approaches

Research on intersectional identities will give more attention to how trauma interacts with the lives of those who have several marginalized identities.

Cultural tailoring: To better meet the requirements of varied groups, trauma-informed care will increasingly employ culturally tailored methods.

Trauma-Informed Laws and Policies

Legislative activism: The future of trauma care will be shaped by ongoing legislative activism for trauma-informed policy at the local, state, and federal levels.

Integration into Education: Healthcare workers, educators, and social service providers may soon be required to complete trauma-informed education.

Early Warning and Prevention

Preventive Programs: More emphasis will be put on creating early intervention tactics and trauma prevention programs, especially in communities and schools.

Building resiliency in people and communities will receive more attention as a preventative tool against the effects of trauma.

Research Objectives

Long-term Results: Studies will increasingly focus on how trauma affects people over the long term, including how it affects their physical and mental health as well as their general well-being.

Trauma in Special Populations: In order to create specialized therapies, research will focus on the trauma experiences of particular populations, such as refugees, veterans, and inmates.

Advancements in genetic and epigenetic research could provide light on how trauma is passed down through generations and its hereditary components.

Innovative approaches to preventing trauma and lessening its effects, such as community-based and policy-level interventions, will be the subject of research on preventive methods.

Communities-Based Methods

Communities will increasingly collaborate to foster resilience and provide survivors with group assistance.

Community-Led projects: Community-led and grassroots projects that are trauma-informed will keep gaining ground.

Environmental and Climate Trauma

Climate Crisis: Trauma-informed care may need to broaden its scope to cover the psychological effects of environmental trauma and disasters linked to the climate.

Ecotherapy: With the growing understanding of the connection between the well-being of the individual and the environment, ecotherapy may be more fully incorporated into trauma treatment.

Conclusion

Innovation, increased accessibility, and a better understanding of the complex and varied experiences of trauma will define the future of trauma-informed care. We can create a more compassionate and efficient approach to healing and rehabilitation for all people and communities affected by trauma by embracing emerging trends, performing significant research, and staying dedicated to the fundamentals of trauma-informed treatment.

Personal And Professional Growth: The Rewards And Challenges Of Working In Trauma-Informed Fields.

Working in trauma-informed fields is rewarding and difficult, whether you're a therapist, educator, healthcare practitioner, or advocate. This chapter examines the personal and professional development that those in these positions go through, stressing the special benefits and potential difficulties.

The Benefits of Working with Trauma

Impactful Healing: It may be tremendously gratifying and affirming to see trauma survivors go through a positive shift and heal.

Building Trust: One rewarding part of trauma-informed work is creating strong, trustworthy bonds with clients, patients, or pupils.

Working in trauma-informed industries gives you the chance to promote systemic change, confront societal inequalities, and help create a more compassionate society.

Personal Development: Professionals frequently grow personally, develop greater empathy, and feel a greater sense of purpose in their profession.

Learning and Professional Development: Work that is informed by trauma requires ongoing learning and professional development to keep practitioners interested and intellectually stimulated.

The Difficulties of Working with Trauma

Emotional Cost: Being exposed to painful tales and powerful emotional experiences can make one more vulnerable to suffering from burnout, compassion fatigue, and vicarious trauma.

Boundary Management: It can be difficult to manage boundaries, remain professional, and still provide sensitive and compassionate care.

Systemic dissatisfaction: When promoting trauma-informed practices and policies within bureaucratic structures, one may encounter opposition and dissatisfaction.

Struggles with Self-Care: Because professionals frequently put the needs of others before their own, it can be challenging to strike a balance between self-care and the obligations of the job.

Professionals may experience secondary trauma, which may have an effect on their personal lives, interpersonal connections, and general well-being.

Methods for Personal and Professional Development

Prioritize self-care activities like practicing mindfulness, working out, and getting help from friends, mentors, or therapists.

Participate in routine supervision or consultation to process difficult issues and get advice on moral conundrums.

Boundaries: To safeguard your emotional wellbeing and uphold professionalism, set clear and healthy boundaries.

Education and Training: To stay up to date with trauma-informed approaches and best practices, invest in ongoing education and training.

Peer Support: Seek assistance from coworkers who are aware of the particular difficulties associated with trauma-informed employment.

Join advocacy networks and groups to meet people who share your enthusiasm for trauma-informed care and social change.

Conclusion

Working in domains that are trauma-informed is a noble and significant activity that can promote both professional and personal development. Professionals may continue to improve the lives of trauma survivors and develop trauma-informed treatment by recognizing and addressing the problems while prioritizing self-care and continual learning.

A Call To Action: Encouraging A Broader Adoption Of Trauma-Informed Practices.

It is crucial to promote the widespread adoption of trauma-informed practices across all sectors and communities as awareness of trauma and trauma-informed care increases. This book's last chapter issues a call to action by highlighting the actions that people, groups, and communities can do to advance and incorporate trauma-informed methodologies into their professional and everyday lives.

1. Training and Education

Continuous Learning: To stay up to speed on best practices, people in all professions should make a commitment to continued education and training in trauma-informed care.

Professional growth: Employers and organizations ought to give trauma-informed training top priority and offer tools so that staff members can advance their abilities.

2. Advocating for policy

Advocate for trauma-informed legislation at the local, state, and federal levels to make sure that institutions and systems give trauma sensitivity top priority.

Encourage legislators and community leaders to work together using trauma-informed approaches to meet the particular needs of their communities.

3. School Integration

Promote the incorporation of trauma-informed

principles into school curricula, teacher preparation programs, and institutional practices.

Promote greater accessibility to mental health services in schools to meet the emotional needs of pupils who have experienced trauma.

4. Healthcare Reform

Changes to the Healthcare System: Advocate for the adoption of trauma-informed care as a routine procedure in the healthcare systems, including education for all healthcare workers.

Support and promote study funding to further examine how trauma affects one's health and well-being.

5. Reform of Criminal Justice

Promote trauma-informed procedures throughout the criminal justice system, including instruction for officers of the law, magistrates, and inmates.

Advocate for the creation and funding of prevention and diversion programs that deal with the underlying reasons of criminal behavior, such as trauma.

6. Participation of the local community

Encourage grassroots and community-led trauma-informed programs that take into account the particular needs of the local population.

Support the creation of community resources like crisis hotlines and support groups for victims of trauma.

7. Services for Mental Health

Increased access to mental health care should be pushed for, especially in impoverished and marginalized populations.

Promote the provision of mental health services that are both culturally competent and culturally adapted.

8. Research and Information Gathering

Support research funding to create an evidence base for effective practices through studying trauma and trauma-informed care.

Encourage the gathering of data on trauma experiences, consequences, and inequities in order to inform practice and policy.

9. Public awareness and the media

Promote appropriate media coverage of trauma-related issues, while also limiting sensationalism and fostering educated discourse.

Support public education initiatives that reduce stigma associated with trauma, mental illness, and seeking assistance.

10. Individual Dedication

Become more trauma-informed in your relationships with others by reflecting on your own actions, behaviors, and biases.

Build and maintain supportive networks with people who share your dedication to trauma-informed ideas.

Conclusion

Trauma-informed care is a revolutionary strategy that has the power to impact the lives of countless people and entire communities. Individuals, groups, and communities must respond to the call to action by promoting and putting trauma-informed strategies into practice in all facets of life in order to fully achieve this potential. Together, we can build a more sympathetic and understanding society that acknowledges the effects of trauma and reacts to it with consideration and empathy.

CONCLUSION

For a compassionate world, embrace trauma-informed care.

We have traveled deeply into the core of human pain and resiliency as a result of our investigation into trauma-informed care. We have examined the intricate web of trauma's effects, listening to survivors' tales and the devoted specialists who assist them. Several overriding themes that have been present throughout our journey have led us to a conclusion that captures the core of trauma-informed care.

The Influence of Understanding and Empathy

Empathy and understanding have the transforming potential at the core of trauma-informed care. We now know that those who have experienced trauma do not require judgment or quick remedies, but rather sympathetic listeners who can accept their suffering without passing judgment. When empathy is practiced in interpersonal interactions on both a personal and professional level, it becomes the basis for healing and rehabilitation.

Understanding Trauma's Widespread Effects

We now understand that trauma has a wide impact that permeates many facets of a person's life. Trauma leaves an irreparable mark, whether it be due to childhood hardship, a fatal accident, or the intangible wounds of war. Trauma is a global condition that affects people of all ages and backgrounds.

The Paradigm Shift to Trauma-Informed Care

A paradigm shift—an awareness of the enormous impact of trauma on people and communities—is represented by trauma-informed treatment. It calls for a more sympathetic, all-encompassing, and human-centered approach to care and challenges conventional models of care. This paradigm shift affects not only healthcare but also criminal justice, education, and society as a whole.

The Path to Resilience and Healing

Our voyage has demonstrated the human spirit's tenacity. People have shown incredible courage and strength in the face of awful hardship. Trauma recovery is a journey marked by ups and downs, failures and successes; it is not a linear process. This is acknowledged by trauma-informed care, which offers a secure, encouraging setting for recovery.

The Request for Action

Our examination of trauma-informed treatment comes to a close with a strong call to action. In every sphere of our society, we must fight for the wider adoption of trauma-informed methods. By establishing areas of safety and support, we must work to eliminate the stigma associated with trauma and mental health. Because it is only through joint effort that we can bring about a more compassionate society, we must unite as allies, supporters, and compassionate people.

In the end, trauma-informed care is more than just a theoretical idea; it's a call to embrace our common humanity and the notion that everyone has a story to tell and that every story deserves to be heard with empathy and understanding. Let's continue to spread this message as we work to create a society where compassion, resiliency, and healing are valued equally.

EPILOGUE

We have descended into the depths of human pain and resiliency in our investigation of trauma-informed care. While we have seen the terrible effects of trauma on people, families, and communities, we have also seen how powerful empathy, understanding, and support can be. It is crucial that we consider the timeless truths and guiding principles as we get to the end of our trip.

Effects of Trauma

Trauma is an unpleasant travel companion for people, impacting people of all ages, races, genders, and socioeconomic backgrounds. It leaves behind wounds that are often invisible but are yet profoundly ingrained in the psyche. It has become clear that trauma affects a person's entire life, from relationships and community interactions to mental and physical health, going well beyond the original occurrence.

Trauma-Informed Care's Promise

But in the midst of the trauma's darkness, we

have found a glimmer of hope: trauma-informed care. This method acknowledges that trauma is an experience that shapes lives rather than just an incident. The healing process places a high value on safety, trust, and empathy, according to trauma-informed care. It serves as a reminder that healing is a process that requires time, patience, and support.

The Human Spirit's Ableness to Survive

We have seen firsthand the incredible resiliency of the human spirit via the perseverance of trauma-informed professionals and the testimonies of survivors. It is a kind of resilience that overcomes obstacles, triumphs over hardship, and finds courage in weakness. It serves as a reminder that despite extreme suffering, there is still room for development, recovery, and change.

The Request for Action

With us as we say goodbye to this examination of trauma-informed treatment is a strong call to action. We have a responsibility to fight for the broad adoption of trauma-informed approaches in our communities, schools, and healthcare and criminal justice systems. By establishing venues that are safe for survivors to express their experiences and look for support, we are asked to combat the stigma associated with trauma and mental health.

Recognizing that the path to recovery and resilience

is a shared one, we are called to stand together as allies, advocates, and compassionate people. We are obligated to promote compassion, empathy, and understanding since it is these traits that have the capacity to change people's lives and revitalize entire communities.

Finally, let's keep in mind that trauma does not define us; rather, it is how we respond to adversity that determines how we will turn out. We set out on a journey of recovery, development, and resiliency with trauma-informed care as our beacon —a journey that offers the promise of a better and more understanding future for all.

Printed in Great Britain
by Amazon

36460972R00076